Bedrock Press™
A T L A N T A
Published by Bedrock Press
An imprint of Turner Publishing, Inc.
A Subsidiary of Turner Broadcasting System, Inc.
1050 Techwood Drive, N. W.
Atlanta, Georgia 30318

Printed in the U. S. A.
First Edition 10 9 8 7 6 5 4 3 2 1
ISBN   1-878685-68-6
Library of Congress Catalog
Card Number 93-61336

Distributed by Andrews and McMeel
A Universal Press Syndicate Company
4900 Main Street, Kansas City,
Missouri 64112

DK DIRECT LIMITED
Managing Art Editor Eljay Crompton
Senior Editor Rosemary Mc Cormick
Consultant Nicholas Booth
Writer Quentin Daniel
Illustrators Hanna-Barbera, Inc.,
Steve Weston, John Dowes, Richard Manning
Designers Diane Klein, Marianne Markham

THE JETSONS
EXPLORE
SPACE

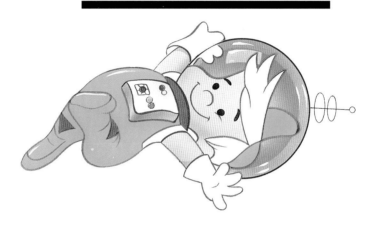

Bedrock Press™
A T L A N T A

"Dear Reader"

This book has been created especially for you. It's guaranteed to provide fun, adventure, and fabulous nuggets of information. From countdown to blast-off, the Jetsons prepare us every step of the way. It may be new to us but the Jetsons have been traveling in space for years! Full-color, detailed pictures give you a whole new view of space life. Every section is full of fun facts. We hope you enjoy this exciting adventure, and we look forward to having you join us on another Fantastic Discovery.

CONTENTS

WE HAVE LIFT-OFF!

Countdown to lift-off! At the Kennedy Space Center, the shuttle is ready to be launched. The Jetsons have zoomed back in time to experience space travel in the twentieth century. Our Jetson crew walks from the launch tower to the shuttle. On board, they will strap themselves into their seats and check the controls. Soon, the ground controller will count off the minutes and seconds to lift-off.

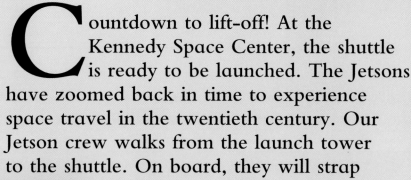

Check it Out!
Standing next to the shuttle is the launch tower. From here the ground crew carefully makes the final checks on the shuttle, which can take up to three days!

Safety First
The launch area is cleared of workers after the crew boards the shuttle. Huge flames and clouds of smoke burst from the end of the rockets at lift-off.

There and Back
The shuttle is a special spacecraft that can go into space, return to Earth, and be relaunched again and again. It is about the size of a large plane. But unlike a plane, the shuttle can take-off straight up into the sky because it has rocket engines.

Big Boosters
Strapped to the sides of a huge fuel tank under the shuttle are two big booster rockets. These rockets allow the shuttle to blast-off into the sky, reaching speeds of more than 3,000 mph!

Rockets were invented in China in the thirteenth century and were used as fireworks and weapons of war. Modern rockets became more powerful when they began to use liquid fuels. This Russian rocket, called Soyuz, was launched in 1967.

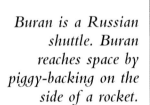

The U.S. Saturn 5 was the biggest rocket ever built. It was about as big as a 10-story building.

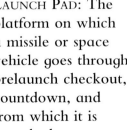

Buran is a Russian shuttle. Buran reaches space by piggy-backing on the side of a rocket.

GROUND CONTROL: The operations center on Earth that monitors and gives instructions to the shuttle crew while in flight.

LAUNCH PAD: The platform on which a missile or space vehicle goes through prelaunch checkout, countdown, and from which it is launched.

MOVING IN SPACE

Ten minutes after lift-off, the shuttle is roaring into space. On board, the Jetsons are recovering from lift-off. Everything has gone according to plan. As the shuttle climbed into space, the rocket boosters and fuel tank were dropped and fell back to Earth. When the shuttle has climbed to 150 miles, it will circle the Earth at a speed of five miles per second. A circle of the Earth is called an orbit.

Heavy Load!
The shuttle's cargo bay can carry two satellites – a weight of about 30 tons. That's about as heavy as 60 elephants!

Taking a Break
When the crew members are not busy with their mission tasks, they spend their time below the flight deck in the living quarters. This is where they eat, sleep, shower – and watch TV!

Two minutes after lift-off the two rocket boosters fall from the shuttle into the Atlantic. They are picked up by a waiting ship. Six minutes later, the empty fuel tank also drops away from the shuttle.

Driving in Space
The cockpit area of the shuttle contains hundreds of switches, instruments, and controls. The crew have spent a long time learning how to use this equipment on a special machine called the shuttle mission simulator.

Who's in Charge?
The flight deck is where the commander, pilot, and two flight engineers operate the four main computers that run the shuttle systems. A fifth computer is used in emergencies.

Engine Power
Helped by the rocket boosters, the shuttle's three rocket engines propel the shuttle out of sight from Earth within one minute after take-off. Once in space, small thruster rockets help the crew adjust its position as it orbits the Earth at 17,000 mph!

The Soviet Yuri Gagarin was the first person to go into space on April 12, 1961.

On May 5, 1961, Alan B. Shephard became the first American to go into space.

On June 18, 1983, Dr. Sally Ride became the first American woman to go into space.

PROPEL: To drive forward; to force ahead.

DOCKING TIME

This is a close-up of Mir's docking area. As many as six spacecraft can dock with Mir at the same time.

Did you know that the Earth weighs as much as 81 moons?

There is no air in space so there's no wind, rain, snow, or clouds. That means there's no weather in space as we know it on Earth.

SPACE STATION: An orbiting, manned structure, that can be used for experimental purposes in space.

The Jetsons have arrived at the Russian space station Mir. (Mir is the Russian word for "peace.") The American shuttle is going to join up with the space station to carry out a joint mission. Mir has been orbiting the Earth since 1986 – but not with the same crew! Every six months a spacecraft is sent up with another crew of cosmonauts – Russian astronauts – inside. The shuttle will need to do a lot of neat moves to dock with the space station.

A Flying Can
Space station Mir is shaped like a large tube or can. It is 46 feet long. The main part of the station was launched in 1986. The remaining modules were carried into space and pieced together there.

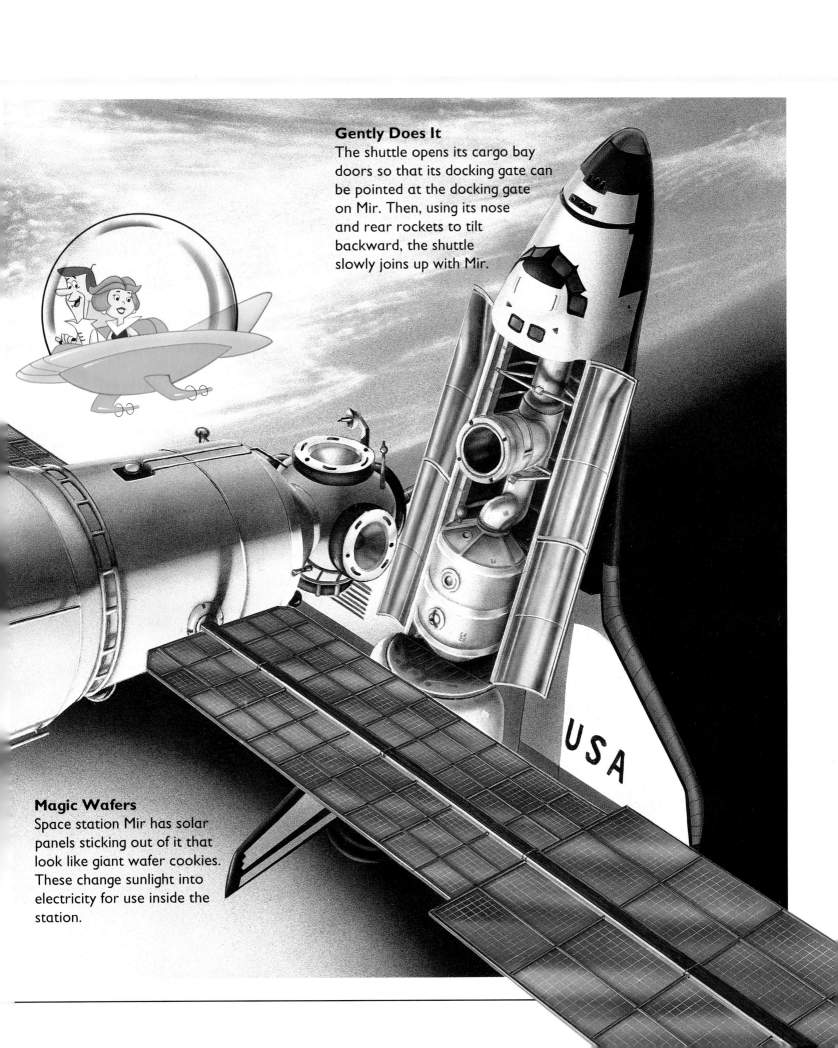

Gently Does It
The shuttle opens its cargo bay doors so that its docking gate can be pointed at the docking gate on Mir. Then, using its nose and rear rockets to tilt backward, the shuttle slowly joins up with Mir.

Magic Wafers
Space station Mir has solar panels sticking out of it that look like giant wafer cookies. These change sunlight into electricity for use inside the station.

WHICH WAY IS UP?

Imagine you are under water. You float around because you don't seem to weigh anything. That's the feeling astronauts have in space because there is no force of gravity to keep them in place. So people are specially trained to live in this weightless world. But, as the Jetsons already know, in the future, space stations will be built so that the lack of gravity isn't a problem – so no more fancy back-flips!

To get used to being in space, astronauts and cosmonauts train in water tanks. They wear weighted suits so they can't sink or float.

Every star would explode into space if its own gravity did not hold it together.

GRAVITY: The natural force that causes objects to move toward the center of a celestial body.

Space Power
Before Russian cosmonauts even push a button, they must lock their feet in footholds. Otherwise, they would shoot backward from the effort!

All Spaced Out!
Without gravity, cosmonauts grow a little taller because the bones in their backs move apart. Also, their faces get puffy because blood goes to their heads. They may also suffer from "space sickness," which is like getting seasick or carsick.

Where's My Onion?
Cosmonauts have successfully grown plants and vegetables in weightless conditions. Once, two cosmonauts were asked to report on the growth of an onion. When they did not, ground control realized that they must have eaten it!

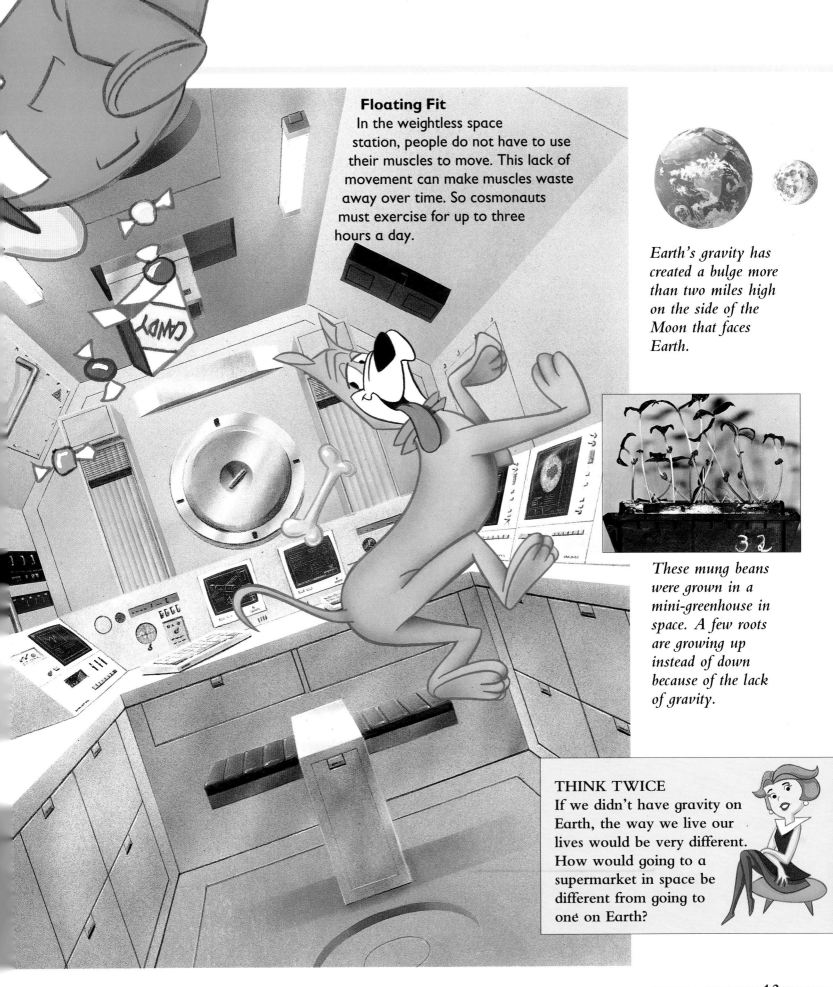

Floating Fit
In the weightless space station, people do not have to use their muscles to move. This lack of movement can make muscles waste away over time. So cosmonauts must exercise for up to three hours a day.

Earth's gravity has created a bulge more than two miles high on the side of the Moon that faces Earth.

These mung beans were grown in a mini-greenhouse in space. A few roots are growing up instead of down because of the lack of gravity.

THINK TWICE
If we didn't have gravity on Earth, the way we live our lives would be very different. How would going to a supermarket in space be different from going to one on Earth?

LIVING IN SPACE

Mir gets its power from the Sun. But it also uses liquid fuel when it needs an extra boost.

Space station Mir is about the size of a large apartment. Russian cosmonauts live in space for several months at a time. During this time they are orbiting the Earth. It may seem a strange thing to do for such a long period – especially when they spend a lot of time floating about. But it is the best way to see how well people can live in space. (On the other hand, they could always ask the Jetsons!)

Flying the Station
The front of Mir contains the control systems. Attached to the floor are instruments for guiding the space station.

Special soda cans have been made that can be carried into space. They have a pressure pump inside that stops the bubbles expanding.

On early missions, cosmonauts had to eat food straight from tubes. Now many foods are served the way they would be on Earth. There's a choice of some 90 food items – including sausages and eggs!

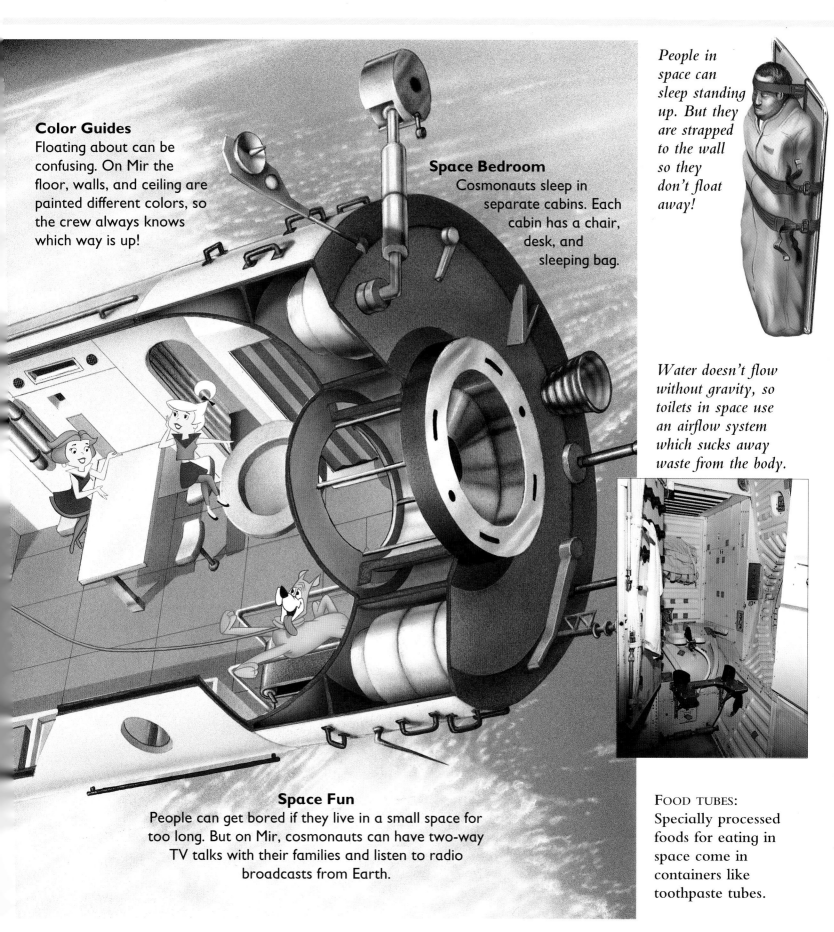

Color Guides
Floating about can be confusing. On Mir the floor, walls, and ceiling are painted different colors, so the crew always knows which way is up!

Space Bedroom
Cosmonauts sleep in separate cabins. Each cabin has a chair, desk, and sleeping bag.

People in space can sleep standing up. But they are strapped to the wall so they don't float away!

Water doesn't flow without gravity, so toilets in space use an airflow system which sucks away waste from the body.

Space Fun
People can get bored if they live in a small space for too long. But on Mir, cosmonauts can have two-way TV talks with their families and listen to radio broadcasts from Earth.

FOOD TUBES: Specially processed foods for eating in space come in containers like toothpaste tubes.

WORKING IN SPACE

A space suit is made of many layers of special material. The space suit itself is in two parts.

Before putting the space suit on, an astronaut puts on water-cooled underwear.

Then the astronaut pulls on the bottom part of the suit.

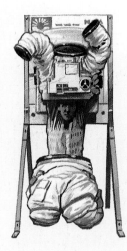

Next, while it is still hanging up, the astronaut slides up into the top part.

SPACEWALK: To move in space without the aid of a vehicle. Space walks are called EVA's, or Extra Vehicular Activities.

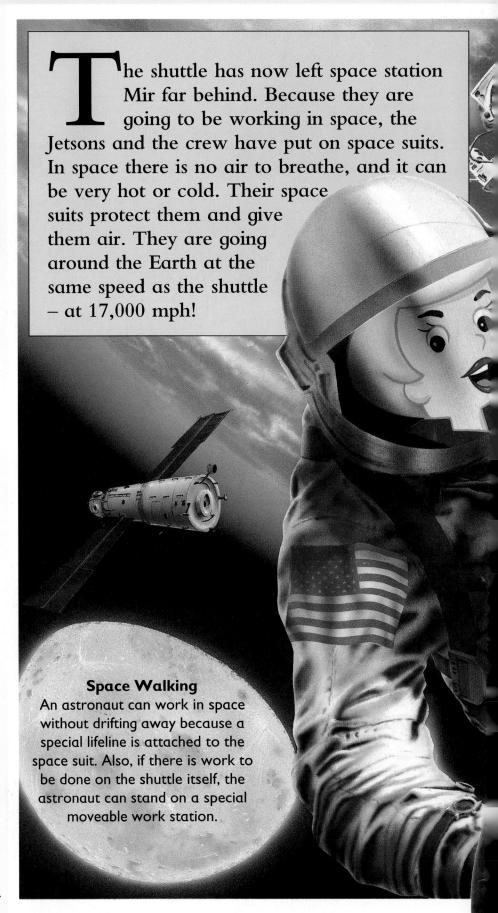

The shuttle has now left space station Mir far behind. Because they are going to be working in space, the Jetsons and the crew have put on space suits. In space there is no air to breathe, and it can be very hot or cold. Their space suits protect them and give them air. They are going around the Earth at the same speed as the shuttle – at 17,000 mph!

Space Walking
An astronaut can work in space without drifting away because a special lifeline is attached to the space suit. Also, if there is work to be done on the shuttle itself, the astronaut can stand on a special moveable work station.

Flying Armchair
To "spacewalk" far from the shuttle, astronauts use a machine called a manned maneuvering unit, or "flying armchair." Small jets of gas push the armchair in the direction the astronaut wants to go.

SPACE DIAPER
Astronauts can go to the bathroom while dressed in their space suits. The suits have a diaper for women and a tube for men.

Super Bowl
A space helmet may look like a fishbowl, but astronauts must wear them to be able to breathe in space. Inside is a microphone and headphones so they can communicate. They also wear a protective cap.

THE MOST AMAZING TELESCOPE

On their voyage, the Jetsons will help repair the Hubble Telescope. This telescope "sends" the images it sees back to Earth in the form of electronic signals. On Earth, the signals are changed into pictures. The Hubble can spot stars in outer space that are 14 billion light years away. So when we look at these pictures, we are seeing the stars as they were 14 billion years ago. In fact, some may no longer exist!

Light Catcher
The Hubble is a 43 foot long tube. It acts as a light trap. Light from distant stars enters the opening in the front and is "caught" inside by mirrors. The light is then directed into a box where it is electronically recorded.

A Clear View

The Hubble is controlled from Earth by signals to its antennae. These signals tell it which way to point. The telescope works 24 hours a day, seven days a week, all year round.

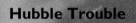

Hubble Trouble

The Hubble contains two mirrors that reflect light from stars and planets. But one of these mirrors is a little too flat — enough to blur all its reflections. So that's why it needs to be repaired!

The Hubble was carried into space by a shuttle in 1990. The telescope was lifted out of the cargo bay by a robotic arm. After its two solar panels had unfolded it was released and the shuttle drew away.

The world's largest solar telescope is on Kitt Peak, in Arizona. The telescope tower stands at 110 feet and the tracking mirror measures five feet across.

Up Close

Because the Hubble Telescope is outside the haze of Earth's atmosphere, it can "see" much more clearly than any Earth-based telescope. And, despite problems, many pictures taken so far have been successful. The distant planet Pluto and its satellite, Charon, have been seen clearly for the first time.

ANTENNA: A device used in transmitting or receiving radio signals.

LIGHT YEAR: The distance traveled by light in one year. Light travels at 186,000 miles per second.

REFLECTION: The throwing back of light or heat.

TELESCOPE: A tube, with lenses and mirrors, to look through that makes distant objects look bigger and closer.

SPACE COMMUNICATION

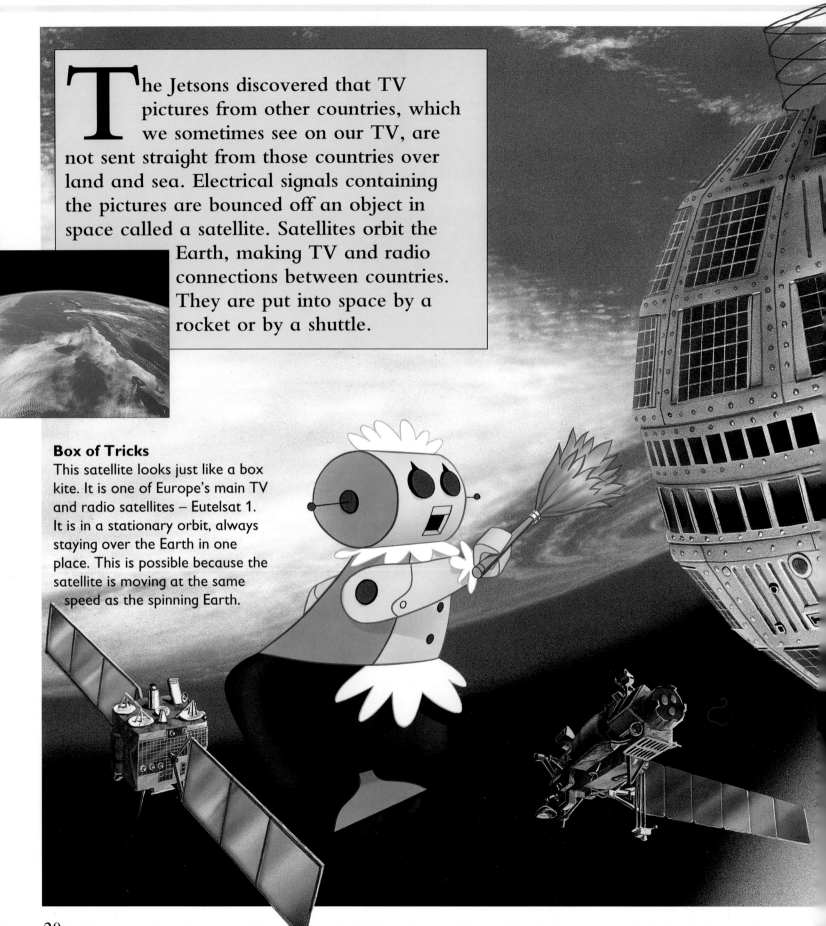

The Jetsons discovered that TV pictures from other countries, which we sometimes see on our TV, are not sent straight from those countries over land and sea. Electrical signals containing the pictures are bounced off an object in space called a satellite. Satellites orbit the Earth, making TV and radio connections between countries. They are put into space by a rocket or by a shuttle.

Box of Tricks
This satellite looks just like a box kite. It is one of Europe's main TV and radio satellites – Eutelsat 1. It is in a stationary orbit, always staying over the Earth in one place. This is possible because the satellite is moving at the same speed as the spinning Earth.

Satellites can move around the Earth in different orbits. Some move in polar orbits – passing over the North and South poles. Others travel high over one side of the Earth and low over the other side.

Meteosat is a satellite that sends back information about the weather.

Geosat is a spy satellite. Spy satellites can "read" the license plate on a car, or truck, from outer space!

Watcher in the Skies

The Earth is protected by a layer of gas called ozone. Many people say the layer is being damaged by chemicals that were used in aerosols and refrigerators. This Upper Atmosphere Research Satellite studies the ozone layer.

Live on TV!

The round Telstar satellite sent the first live TV pictures to and from Europe and the U.S. in 1962. It is very small – only three feet across. Telstar is covered with solar panels.

SATELLITE: A small object, either natural or man-made, that circles around a larger object.

GOING HOME

After eight days in space, it's time to head for Earth. At 25 times the speed of sound, the Jetsons zoom toward Earth's atmosphere. When the shuttle hits the outer layer of the atmosphere the Jetsons must maneuver it carefully since it becomes a huge, swooping glider. When it passes through the atmosphere, the shuttle glows red hot, but it doesn't burn up as it has a special heat shield.

Swooping shuttle re-entering the Earth's atmosphere.

Stratosphere

Ozone

Troposphere

The Earth's atmosphere can be divided up into layers of gases. The ozone layer begins between 10 and 15 miles above the Earth.

ATMOSPHERE: A blanket of gases that surrounds the Earth or any other celestial body.

RE-ENTRY: The return of a spacecraft into the Earth's atmosphere.

Flying Brickyard
The shuttle is often called "The Flying Brickyard." This is because it is covered with 33,000 ceramic tiles, which soak up heat and protect the shuttle and crew from burning up.

Heavy Glider
The wings of the shuttle are in a "delta" triangular shape. This shape is ideal for gliding. At 98 tons, the shuttle is surely the heaviest glider ever built!

No Turning Back

Once the astronauts have put the shuttle on the path to re-entry, they cannot change their minds. This is because there is not enough fuel in its main engines for a second try.

Red Hot

The underside of the shuttle builds up the most heat during re-entry. It can reach as high as 3,500° F – that's about 15 times as hot as the inside of Mom's oven!

Each shuttle tile is like no other, and has to be carefully glued in its own particular place – by hand!

Blackout!

As the shuttle re-enters the Earth's atmosphere, there is what is called a "blackout" in its radio links with ground control. This means that for about 15 minutes there is no communication between ground control and the shuttle.

WE HAVE TOUCHDOWN!

Touchdown in 10 seconds! The shuttle has come safely through the Earth's atmosphere and is gliding down toward the Arizona desert. From the flight deck, George and Judy steer the shuttle by controlling the rudder and wing flaps from the cockpit. Once they have landed, they will be questioned by ground control. Then they will be taken to a newsroom to talk to the world about their amazing mission.

Space Shuttle

Aircraft

The shuttle swoops down to land at an angle about four times steeper than an airplane.

RUDDER:
A vertical blade at the stern of a vessel or craft that can be turned to change the vessel's direction while in motion.

SPEED OF SOUND:
A sound wave travels through the air at 741 mph.

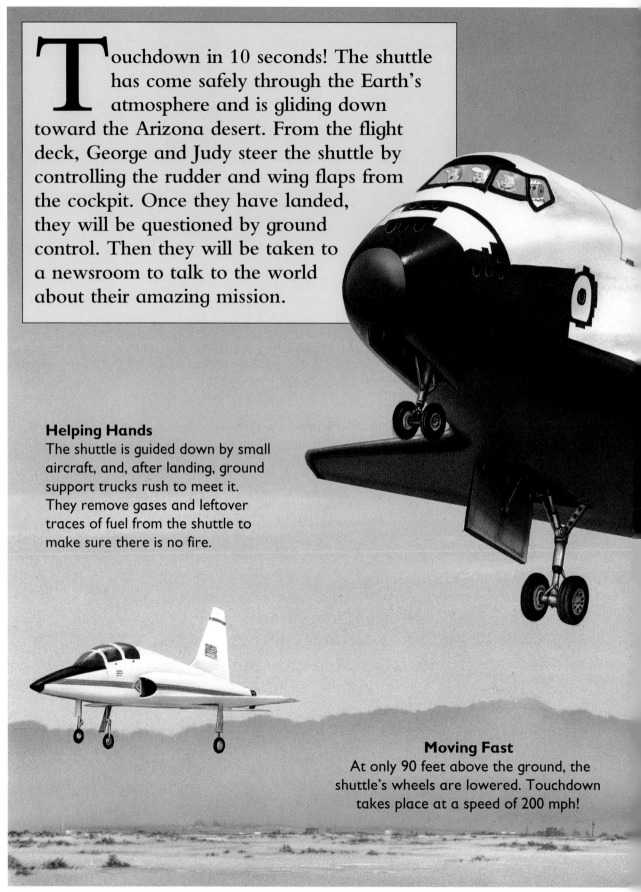

Helping Hands
The shuttle is guided down by small aircraft, and, after landing, ground support trucks rush to meet it. They remove gases and leftover traces of fuel from the shuttle to make sure there is no fire.

Moving Fast
At only 90 feet above the ground, the shuttle's wheels are lowered. Touchdown takes place at a speed of 200 mph!

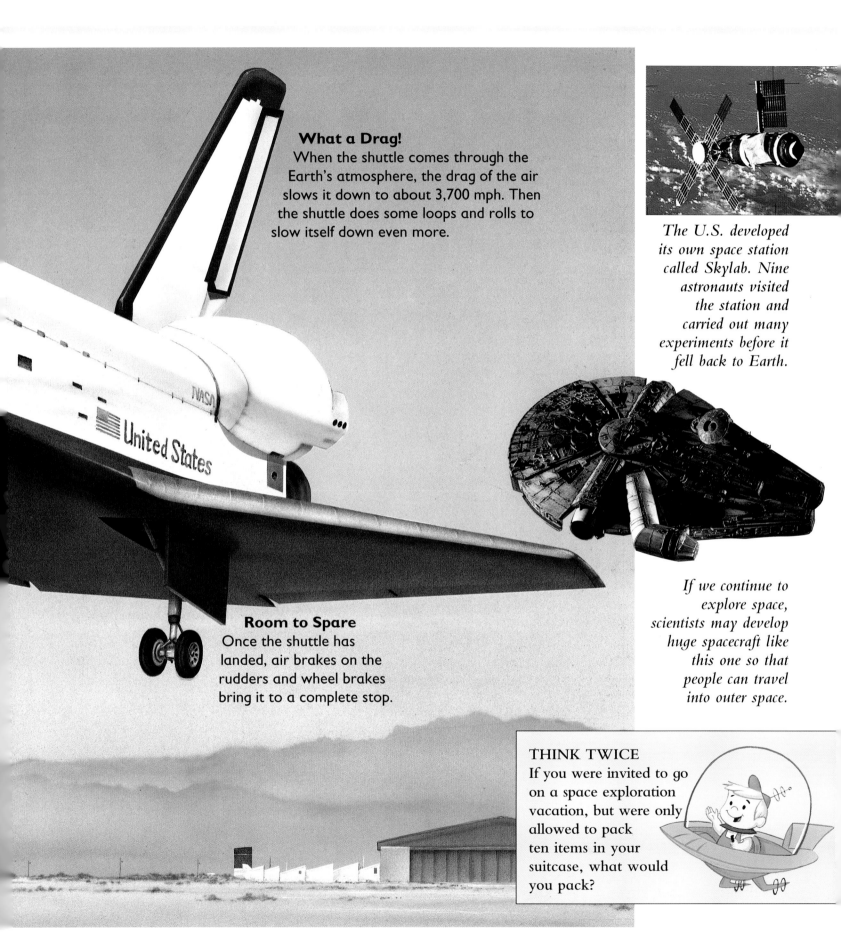

What a Drag!
When the shuttle comes through the Earth's atmosphere, the drag of the air slows it down to about 3,700 mph. Then the shuttle does some loops and rolls to slow itself down even more.

The U.S. developed its own space station called Skylab. Nine astronauts visited the station and carried out many experiments before it fell back to Earth.

Room to Spare
Once the shuttle has landed, air brakes on the rudders and wheel brakes bring it to a complete stop.

If we continue to explore space, scientists may develop huge spacecraft like this one so that people can travel into outer space.

THINK TWICE
If you were invited to go on a space exploration vacation, but were only allowed to pack ten items in your suitcase, what would you pack?

BRAINSTORM

ADVENTURES IN SPACE

Just guess what the missing word or words are to complete the story:
Ten, 9, 8, 7, 6, 5, 4, 3, 2, 1, we have------ . On board the---------- the Jetson crew are getting used to space travel in the twentieth century. After the shuttle has climbed to ---- --------, it begins to ------- the Earth.

The Jetsons will meet up with the --------- space crew on board space station----- . There they will explore the space station and carry out repairs on the --------- --------- . Before returning home, they will also check out some ----------- . Finally, the shuttle will pass through the Earth's ------- before landing safely.

THINK TANK
How would you like to live on a space station? Think about what jobs you would do, and how you would relax. What things would you miss about Earth?

Night Sky
You see it at night.
You also see it during the day.
It is not made of green cheese.
What is it?

WARM RAYS
It is really is VERY hot. It is really a star. We cannot live without it. What is it?

WHAT IF?
What would you do if you woke up one morning and an alien from another planet was sitting in your bedroom?

United States

QUESTION TIME

Why are modern rockets more powerful than the original ones invented by the Chinese?

What is the blanket of gases that surround the Earth called?

Can you remember three different kinds of satellites and what they are used for?

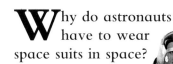

Why can a telescope in space "see" more clearly than one on Earth?

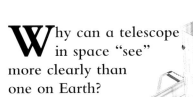

Why do astronauts have to wear space suits in space?

Why are Mir's walls and ceilings painted different colors?

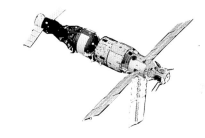

There's a space-age word for circling the Earth – what is it?

Close your eyes and see if you can remember in which part of the space station you would find Mir's controls.

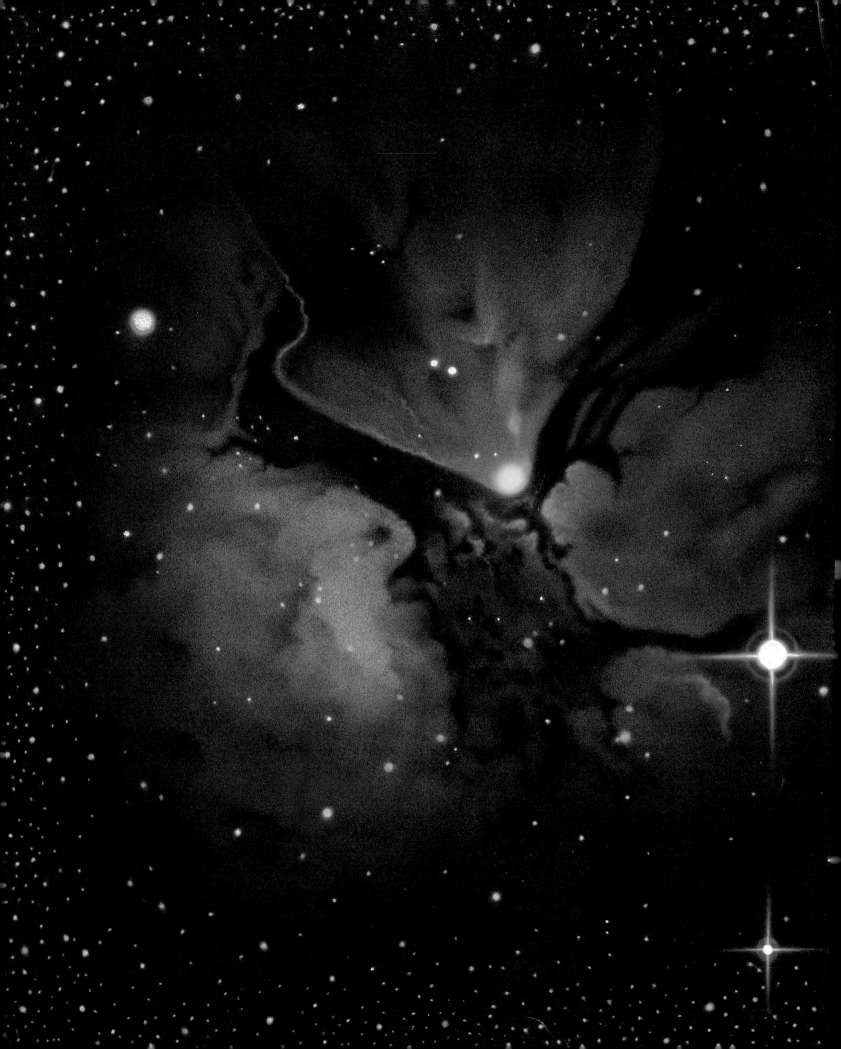